Why do plants have flowers?

Louise and Richard Spilsbury

www.heinemann.co.uk/library

Visit our website to find out more information about Heinemann Library books.

To order:

☎ Phone 44 (0) 1865 888066

📄 Send a fax to 44 (0) 1865 314091

💻 Visit the Heinemann Bookshop at www.heinemann.co.uk/library to browse our catalogue and order online.

First published in Great Britain by Heinemann Library, Halley Court, Jordan Hill, Oxford OX2 8EJ, part of Harcourt Education. Heinemann is a registered trademark of Harcourt Education Ltd.

Editorial: Kate Bellamy
Design: Jo Hinton-Malivoire and AMR
Illustration: Art Construction
Picture Research: Ruth Blair and Kay Altwegg
Production: Severine Ribierre

Originated by Repro Multi Warna
Printed and bound in China by South China Printing Company

Our thanks to Patsy Dyer for her assistance in the preparation of this book.

The paper used to print this book comes from sustainable resources

ISBN 978 0 431 01806 5
10 09 08 07
10 9 8 7 6 5 4 3 2

British Library Cataloguing in Publication Data

Spilsbury, Louise and Richard
Why do plants have flowers? – (World of plants)
575.6

A full catalogue record for this book is available from the British Library.

Acknowledgements

The Publishers would like to thank the following for permission to reproduce photographs: Corbis pp. **17** (Michael Boys), **20** (Gary Braasch), **10/11** (Jose Fuste Raga), **004b** (Garden Picture Library/James Guilliam), **6**, **13** (Michael and Patricia Fogden), **5a** (Mary Ann McDonald), **4a** (Maurice Nimmo/FLPA), **5b** (Ron Watts), **15**, **19**, **21**; Getty Images p . **18** (Photodisc); OSF p. **16** (photolibrary.com); Science Photo Library pp. **8**, **12**, **14** (Dr Jeremy Burgess), **23** (Dr John Brachenbury), **9** (Martin Land), **26** (Robert Landau), **25** (Calude Nuridsany and Maria Perennou), **22** (Philippe Psaila), **24** (Gregory K. Scott), **30** (Nik Wheeler), **28** (Claude Woodruff).

Cover photograph of an Alpine Longhorn Beetle (*Rosalia alpina*) on a flower reproduced with permission of FLPA/Silvestris Fotoservice.

Find out more about plants at
www.heinemannexplore.co.uk

Contents

Words appearing in the text in bold,
like this, are explained in the Glossary.

What are flowers for?

Lots of plants grow bright, colourful flowers. Flowers make **seeds**. Seeds grow into new plants.

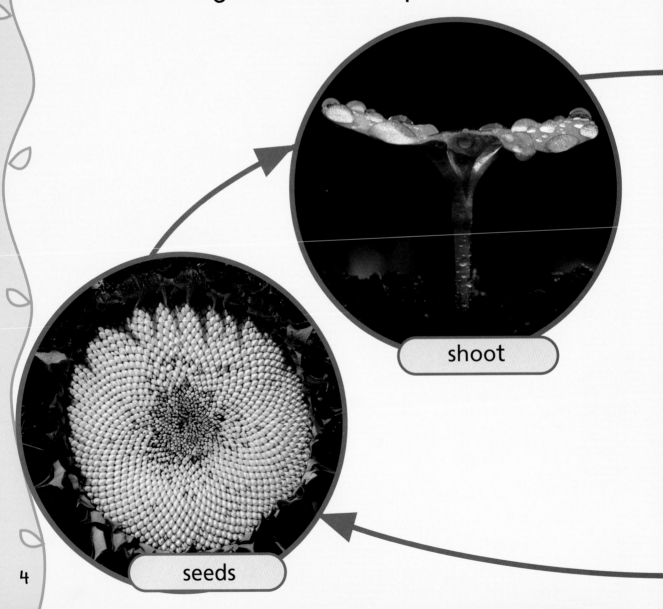

shoot

seeds

Plants and animals have young that grow up to be like them. This is called **reproduction**. Cats have kittens, birds lay eggs and most plants make seeds.

bud

flower

Parts of a flower

There are lots of different parts to a flower. If we cut a flower in half, we can see the parts inside it. The flower uses these parts to make **seeds**.

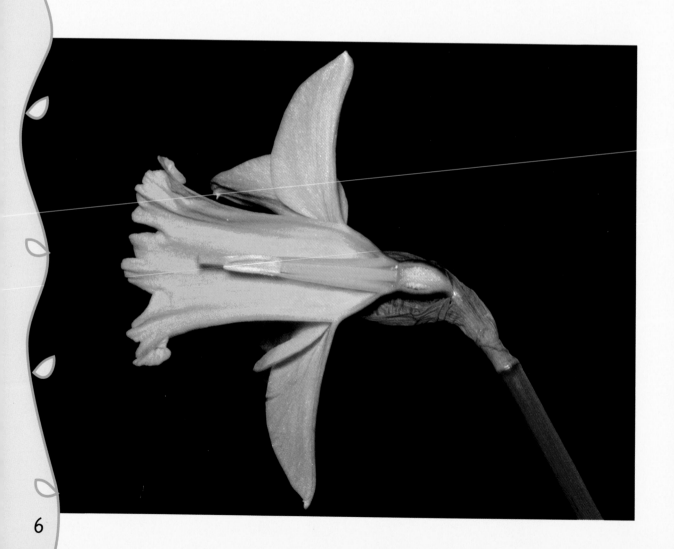

A flower has male and female parts. The male parts are called **stamens**. The female part is called the **carpel**.

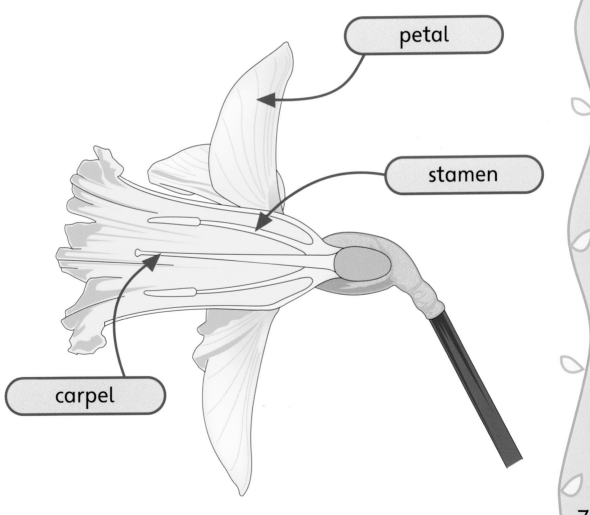

petal

stamen

carpel

Seeds and flowers

Different parts of the flower help to make the **seeds**. At the top of a **stamen** is a kind of powder. This is **pollen**. Pollen is often yellow but it can be other colours, too.

pollen

The female part of a flower makes small grains called **ovules**. You cannot see the ovules on a flower because they are inside the **carpel**.

carpel

pollen

Pollen on the move

In most flowers, a **seed** starts to grow when **pollen** joins with an **ovule**. The pollen moves from one flower to land on another flower.

Only pollen from a poppy can make seeds in another poppy flower.

Different plants have different ways of moving pollen between flowers. Plants cannot move far themselves. So, they have to use what is around them.

Picking up pollen

Some plants use animals to move their **pollen**. Flowers often smell nice and have colourful **petals**. Flowers make a sugary **nectar** drink. This attracts insects and birds.

Some flowers have very long petals. The hummingbird has a very long beak to reach the nectar inside.

Some birds and insects visit flowers to drink the nectar. When a bird or insect comes to drink the nectar, pollen rubs onto their body. When they land on a new flower, the pollen rubs off again.

pollen

Blowing on the wind

Some plants use the wind to move their **pollen**. Their **stamens** make a lot of pollen. The wind blows it. Some of the pollen will land on the **carpel** of a new flower.

A lot of this pollen will fall on the ground and be wasted.

Grass pollen is blown by the wind. The flowers of a grass plant are not brightly coloured and they do not smell. They do not need to attract insects of birds.

Grass flowers are green and dull.

grass flower

A seed starts to grow

When **pollen** lands on the **carpel** of a new flower, it can join with an **ovule**. Then the ovule starts to grow into a **seed**. The **petals** of the flower die and fall off.

The ovule is all that is left of the flower. The seeds inside it grow and get bigger. The ovule slowly swells up around the seeds and it becomes a **fruit**.

The red swellings on this rose bush hold the growing seeds.

17

A fruit forms

A **fruit** is the part of a plant that holds its **seeds**. The fruit keeps the seeds safe while they grow. Some fruits have only one seed.

A cherry is a fruit that has one seed inside.

Some fruits have many seeds inside.
If you cut open a tomato you can
see lots of tiny seeds.

seed

Kinds of fruit

There are many different kinds of **fruit**. Some fruits are soft and juicy and sweet. Some fruits are dry and hard.

fruit

Nuts have a hard, dry fruit around them.

A bean pod is a kind of fruit.
The pod is a case to protect
the **seeds** inside.

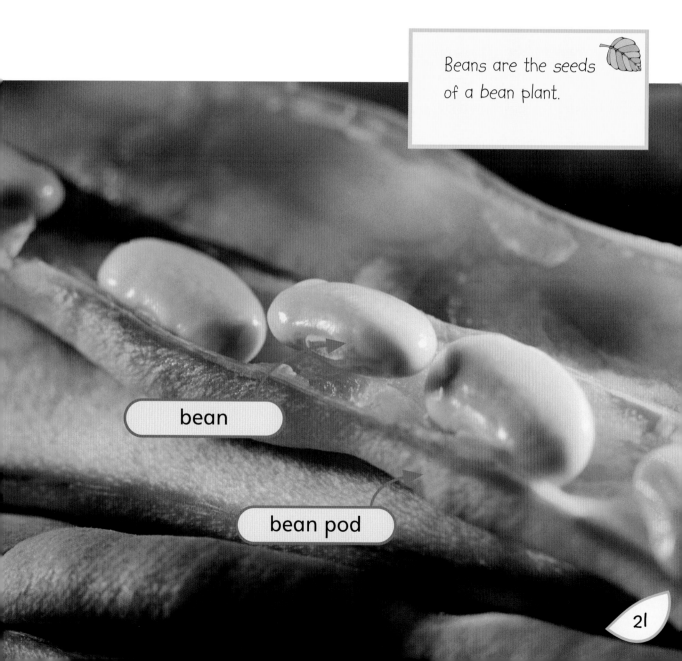

Beans are the seeds
of a bean plant.

bean

bean pod

Fruit and *seeds*

Seeds need space to grow. A **fruit** helps its seeds move away from the parent plant. Some fruits are shaped so they can blow in the wind.

Some seeds are a special shape so that they are blown by the wind.

seed

Some plants use the river to move their seeds to a new place where they can start to grow. Dandelion seeds are very light so they do not sink when they land on water.

seed

Animals and fruits

Animals help to move **seeds**, too. Some animals eat **fruits**. The seeds come out in their **droppings** somewhere new.

Birds may spit out the seeds in a new place.

Some seeds have tiny little hooks on them. These catch onto fur when an animal brushes past the plant. Later the animal rubs the seeds off.

seed

From seed to flower

Some **seeds** land in places where it is too cold or dry for them to grow. Other seeds land in places where they can start to grow.

Seeds falling from this tree will not be able to grow here.

First, a seed lands on new ground. Then, the seed starts to grow into a new plant. One day it will grow its own flowers and seeds.

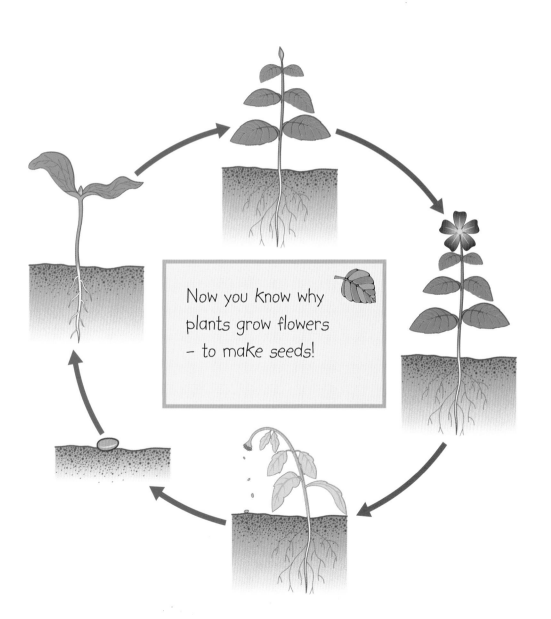

Now you know why plants grow flowers – to make seeds!

Try it yourself!

How many **seeds** do different **fruits** hold? To find out, first collect some different fruits. Then, ask an adult to cut them open for you. Count the seeds inside.

Make a chart like this to show the different number of seeds in each piece of fruit.

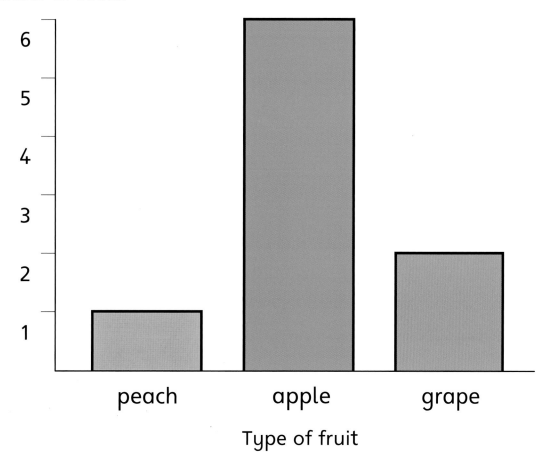

Number of seeds

Type of fruit

Amazing plants!

The seeds of the coco-de-mer tree are probably the biggest in the world! They can weigh up to 20 kilograms (45 pounds) each. That is as heavy as 20 bags of sugar!

 Find out more about plants at
www.heinemannexplore.co.uk

Glossary

carpel female part of a flower

droppings solid waste produced by animals

fruit part of a plant that holds its seeds

nectar sweet sugary juice in the middle of a flower

ovule tiny grain inside the carpel of a flower

petal part of a flower

pollen small grains at the end of a flower's stamen

reproduction when living things produce young (babies) that grow up to be like them

rots when something old or dead breaks down into very, very tiny pieces

seed plant part made by flowers. Seeds can grow to make a new plant.

stamen male part of a flower

More books to read

Life cycles: Broad Bean, Louise Spilsbury, (Raintree, 2003).

Nature's Patterns: Plant Life Cycles, Anita Ganeri (Heinemann Library, 2005).

Plants: Flowers, Patricia Whitehouse (Raintree, 2003).

Index

Titles in the *World of Plants* series include:

Hardback   0 431 01804 9

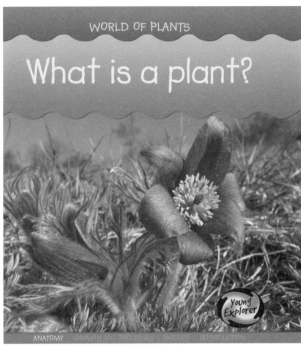

Hardback   0 431 01803 0

Hardback   0 431 01805 7

Hardback   0 431 01806 5

Find out about other titles from Heinemann Library on our website www.heinemann.co.uk/library